READ, TALK & CREATE!

Picture Book Prompts & Imaginative Art Projects for Building Literacy & Communication Skills

by Pamela K. Hill

illustrated by
Vanessa Countryman

Publisher
Key Education Publishing Company, LLC
Minneapolis, Minnesota

www.keyeducationpublishing.com

CONGRATULATIONS ON YOUR PURCHASE OF A KEY EDUCATION PRODUCT!

The editors at Key Education are former teachers who bring experience, enthusiasm, and quality to each and every product. Thousands of teachers have looked to the staff at Key Education for new and innovative resources to make their work more enjoyable and rewarding. We are committed to developing educational materials that will assist teachers in building a strong and developmentally appropriate curriculum for young children.

PLAN FOR GREAT TEACHING EXPERIENCES WHEN YOU USE EDUCATIONAL MATERIALS FROM KEY EDUCATION PUBLISHING COMPANY, LLC

About the Author

With a BA degree in French and a minor in art history and an MA in museum studies with concentrations in art history and education, Pamela K. Hill worked as an art museum educator before beginning her career in educational publishing. As a product developer and an acquisitions editor, she designed and wrote many posters, games, and other teaching tools for preschool and elementary students and teachers. She also helped authors develop their own teacher resource books. *Read, Talk & Create!* is her first book. Pamela lives in North Carolina with her husband and two young sons.

Dedication

To Zachary and Nicholas—I look forward to many years of reading, talking, and creating with both of you.

Credits

Author: Pamela K. Hill
Publisher: Sherrill B. Flora
Illustrator: Vanessa Countryman
Editors: Debra Olson Pressnall & Karen Seberg
Cover Production: Annette Hollister-Papp
Page Layout: Debra Olson Pressnall
Cover Photographs: © Shutterstock, © Comstock
    & Annette Hollister-Papp
Child's Art (Fish) on Cover: Katie

Key Education welcomes manuscripts and product ideas from teachers. For a copy of our submission guidelines, please visit our Web site or send a self-addressed, stamped envelope to:

Key Education Publishing Company, LLC
Acquisitions Department
7309 West 112th Street
Minneapolis, Minnesota 55438

Table of Contents

Introduction

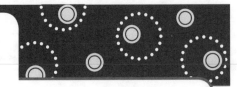

Picture books are an essential part of any early childhood or primary classroom because they open doors to many topics through their pictures and words. *Read, Talk & Create!* offers engaging lessons for 21 different picture books to teach skills and concepts for both literacy and art. With the discussion prompts and easy-to-complete art projects, teachers can build oral language while strengthening young children's thinking processes. During the lessons, students communicate about what is read to them—in verbal form through group discussions and informal presentations, in written form through simple writing or dictation projects, and in visual form through art in various media. In addition, the imaginative projects build fine and gross motor skills as children learn to manipulate a variety of fun art materials. As your students complete the activities in this resource book, keep the following tips in mind:

Tips for Reading and Building Conversations

- Preview each picture book on your own while looking at the suggested questions and prompts for discussion so that you know what to expect when reading the selected book with your students.
- While reading to your students, be sure to direct as much attention to the book's illustrations as to its text. In picture books, the pictures are often as important to telling the story as the words!
- In many cases, you may only want to page through the book with your students before reading it and asking the discussion questions. This will help your students experience the book as a whole before beginning a more in-depth exploration. There are some books that may be exceptions where predicting is an important part of the story, and this is noted as needed for each book.
- While working on the art project related to each book, have the book available for students to review as they wish.
- After you read a book with your students, place it in your classroom library so that students can look at and read it during independent center time.

Tips for Creative Art Projects

- While these projects are designed to be simple and appropriate for preschool and kindergarten children, there are many that may be messy! Supply smocks or have children bring old, oversized shirts from home to use as paint shirts.
- Use washable art materials (paints, crayons, markers, and so on) whenever possible to make cleanup easier.
- Read the entire project thoroughly before beginning and be sure to have all listed materials available.
- Make a sample project or, if you have a young child not in your class to work with you, have the child make a sample project.

- The focus of each of these art projects is on the process and ideas, not the product. Give students the freedom to create what they want within the guidelines of the project.
- Art, writing, and speaking work together as three different forms of communication. Encourage students to talk and write about the art they have created even beyond the guidelines in the Speaking, Writing & Sharing portion of each chapter.
- Collect materials that can be used for art experiences—yogurt containers can substitute for cups to hold paint or water, paper scraps of all types can be used for collages, and certain activities call for specific recycled materials. If you know you will need particular scrap or recycled materials for a project, send a note to parents in advance asking for their help in collecting the items.

Glossary of Art Concepts & Skills

assemblage—a three-dimensional collage; a sculpture made of various materials, often found objects or scraps, attached together

collaboration—two or more artists working to create an artwork

collage—a picture or design created by attaching mostly flat materials, often found objects or scraps, to a flat surface; derived from the French word *coller*, which means "to paste"

printmaking—creating artwork by making an image on a surface using a wet material, and then pressing a flat object, such as paper or fabric, on that surface to transfer the image

role-play/performance—acting out a situation or story

Tips for Speaking, Writing & Sharing

- Model talking about each project for children using your sample project. This demonstration is an opportunity to present vocabulary or ideas you would like students to incorporate into their own presentations.
- Let students present their artwork to the class. There may not be opportunities for every child to talk about every project during the school year, but be sure to carve out some time for each student to share a selected work over a period of several projects.
- For students who are not yet writing on their own, you or a classroom volunteer can take dictation from them to allow them to complete their writing projects.
- When a writing template is provided for a project, you may want to make a transparency of the template or write the template's contents on chart paper. Then, you and your students can fill out the template together as a model for their individual pieces of writing.

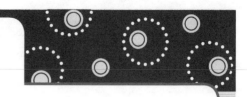

Chicka Chicka Boom Boom

Written by Bill Martin Jr. and John Archambault
Illustrated by Lois Ehlert

New York: Simon and Schuster Books for Young Readers, 1989

Literacy Concepts and Skills

- Identifying details
- Identifying letter formations
- Predicting
- Rhyming
- Speaking
- Spelling
- Vocabulary—(names, descriptions) tag-along K, skinned-knee D, stubbed-toe E, patched-up F, H tangled up with I, J/K about to cry, L knotted like a tie, M looped, N stooped, O twisted alley-oop, black-eyed P, loose-tooth T

Story Summary

The letter *a* challenges the rest of the alphabet to join it in a climb up the coconut tree, but read to see what happens when all of those letters reach the top of the tree! This alphabet book aids in letter identification through fun rhythm and rhyme, while its bright, simple, paper artwork adds to its appeal.

Art Concepts and Skills

- Assemblage
- Color
- Sculpture

Reading & Building Conversation

As you share the book with your class, use the following questions and prompts to encourage discussion and build oral language skills:

- What does the letter *a* tell the other letters to do?
- Most pages in this book contain rhymes using both letters and words. Have children identify rhymes as you read.
- After you have read the question "Chicka chicka boom boom! Will there be enough room?" ask the children if they think there will be enough room in the coconut tree for all of the letters.
- As you read aloud the letters in the text of the book, you may wish to have a student come forward and point out the illustration of the letter as you read about it.
- When you reach the page that says "The whole alphabet up the—Oh, no!" ask the children to predict what they think happens on the next page and then explain their thoughts to a classmate who is sitting nearby.

Creative Art Project

My Name on the Coconut Tree Sculpture

Materials
Letter Patterns (pages 8 and 9)
card stock in assorted bright colors
paper towel tubes, one for each student
construction paper in assorted shades of green and
  brown
scissors, school glue, paper plates (coated), and pencils

Process
Look at a class roster to figure out how many of each upper- and lowercase letter you will need for all of your students' first names. Then, make the necessary number of copies of the reproducible letter patterns on assorted bright colors of card stock. Cut the letter squares apart or have your students do it.

Give each child a cardboard tube, a pair of scissors, and a blob of school glue on a small paper plate. Also, provide access to the colorful letters and green and brown construction paper. Explain to students that they are going to create coconut tree sculptures with the letters in their names climbing up the trees' trunks. Demonstrate how to use fingers to spread a thin layer of glue on the paper pieces and then press them firmly onto the cardboard tube. Students may draw and cut out coconut tree leaves from the green paper and glue them to the tops of their paper towel tubes. Then, they should draw and cut out coconuts

from the brown paper and glue them among the leaves on their trees. Finally, show the children the colorful letters. Explain that they will find the letters in their names and glue them to the cardboard tubes so that their names are climbing up their trees' trunks.

Children should choose uppercase for the first letter in their names and lowercase for the remaining letters. Before they begin, have them lay out their letters on a flat surface so that you can verify that they have selected the correct letters. Alternatively, let students cut out the letters along the heavy black lines so that they are letter-shaped. When they are done gluing, help the children place their trees on their sides in a safe place to dry.

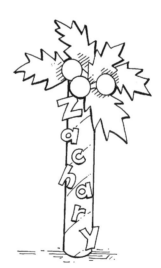

Speaking, Writing & Sharing

Once the trees have dried, create a "Chicka Chicka Boom Boom" class coconut tree grove by stapling the tree trunks to a bulletin board. Label the board "Look Who Are Climbing up the Coconut Trees!" Using a digital camera, photograph each child separately and print a copy of it.

Gather your students in front of the display and work with them to recognize their classmates' names. As they identify a name, invite that child to come forward to name each letter and its color and then attach her photo near the corresponding tree.

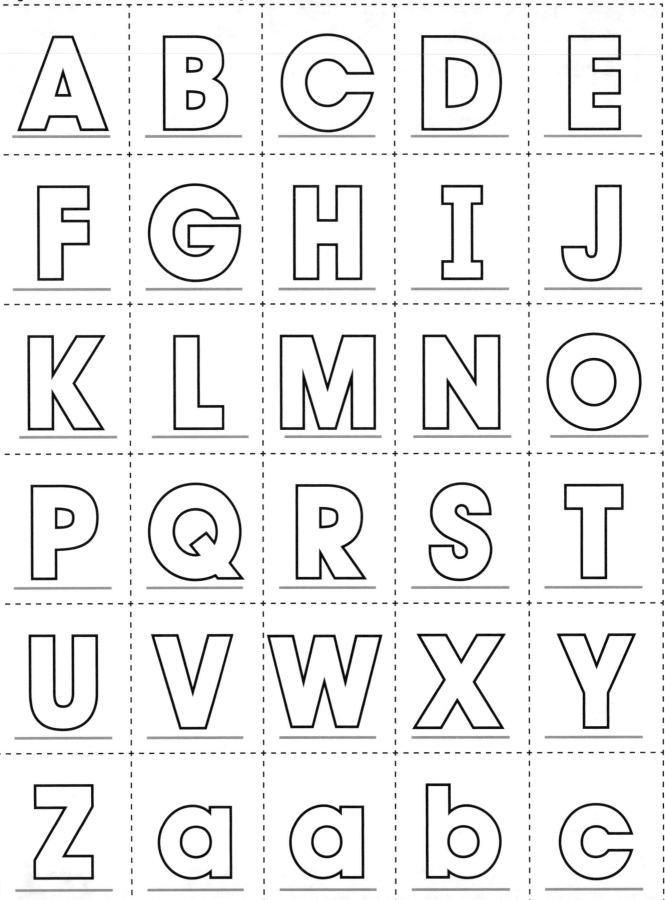

My Name on the Coconut Tree Sculpture—Letter Patterns (Blank cards for more letters)

d	e	e	f	g
h	i	i	j	k
l	m	n	o	o
p	q	r	s	t
u	u	v	w	x
y	z			

Corduroy

Written and illustrated by Don Freeman

New York: The Viking Press, 1968

Literacy Concepts and Skills

- Describing
- Sequencing
- Speaking
- Writing

Art Concepts and Skills

- Collage
- Color

Story Summary

Corduroy is a stuffed bear who lives in a large department store. A little girl wants to buy him, but her mother notices that a button is missing from his overalls. After the store closes, he goes on a nighttime adventure through the department store looking for his missing button. The next day, the little girl returns to buy him and take him home to be her friend. Once they are home, she repairs his missing button so that he can be more comfortable. At the end of the book, Corduroy is happy to have found a friend and a home.

Reading & Building Conversation

As you share the book with your class, use the following questions and prompts to encourage discussion and build oral language skills:

- Where in the department store does Corduroy live?
- What kind of clothing does Corduroy wear?
- Why doesn't the little girl's mother want to buy Corduroy for her daughter?
- What places in the department store does Corduroy visit as he looks for his missing button? Have students name the places in order.
- What happens the day after Corduroy goes looking for his missing button?
- What does Corduroy's new home look like? Where will he be sleeping there?
- How do you think Corduroy and Lisa feel at the end of the book?

Creative Art Project

Dressing Your Bear Friend

Materials

Bear Cutout Pattern (page 12)
brown construction paper
collage materials—assorted fabric and paper scraps,
   buttons, ribbons, yarn, etc.
paper plates (coated)
school glue
scissors

Process

Reproduce one bear cutout on brown construction paper for each student and cut the bears out, or have students cut them out. Supply enough scissors, glue on paper plates, and collage materials for your students to share. Explain that the bears are their new friends, just like Corduroy was the little girl's new friend. Discuss what different articles of clothing they may want to dress their bears in before they begin. Then, let the children cut out collage materials to make the clothes and paste them onto their bears.

Speaking, Writing & Sharing

Once students have finished their bears and the glue has dried, return the bears to the children. Give each child a copy of the Dressing My Bear writing template (page 13). Have the student "write" or dictate the bear's name in the first box on the template, the word *He* or *She* in the second box, and the name and color of some of the clothing the bear is wearing in the third box. When everyone is finished with the writing task, display the bears on a department store shelf bulletin board. Use brown paper to create "shelves" and position the bears so that they look like they are sitting on them. Let the children take turns "reading" their papers and talking about the bears on the store shelves.

● ● ● **12** ● ● ●

Name:

Dressing My Bear

My bear's name is

.

(He/She)

is wearing

.

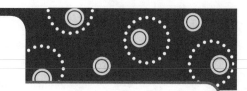

David's Drawings

Written and illustrated by Cathryn Falwell

New York: Lee & Low Books, 2001

Literacy Concepts and Skills

- Comparing and contrasting
- Describing
- Predicting
- Sequencing
- Speaking

Art Concepts and Skills

- Collaboration
- Drawing

Story Summary

David sees a tree on the way to school. He starts to draw it, and, while he is working, several of his classmates make suggestions of things to add. He completes a few of the additions himself and lets some of them add to the drawing, too. Soon, many more children in the class have added their ideas to David's drawing. David recognizes that it really isn't his drawing anymore but the class's drawing. He labels it as such and hangs it on a bulletin board in the room. Then, when he gets home, he makes another drawing of the tree. This time, he keeps it as is and labels it as his own. This book presents a great lesson about collaboration while also valuing individual achievements.

Reading & Building Conversation

As you share the book with your class, use the following questions and prompts to encourage discussion and build oral language skills:

- What does David see on his way to school? What does he do when he arrives at school?
- What does David use to create his drawing?
- How many other children add to David's drawing? What are some of the things they add?
- Who adds the first thing? Who adds the last thing?

- How would you feel if your friends added a bunch of things to a drawing you had made?
- On the way home from school, David sees the tree again. What do you think he will do when he gets home?
- After David draws the tree again, his sister says she thinks it needs something. What do you think she is going to suggest?
- How is the drawing David does at home like the drawing he and his friends did at school? How are the two drawings different?

Creative Art Project

Group and Individual Drawings

Materials

large piece of white chart paper
colored index card labeled with the words "your turn to draw"
list of students' names in the order you want them to draw
colored index card or sentence strip
black marker
pencil
crayons
one sheet of 11" x 17" (28 cm x 43 cm) white paper for each student

Process

For this project, the class will create one large group drawing, like the one David and his classmates made in the book. Then, students will each make an individual drawing of the same subject.

Work with students to choose a subject for the drawings. You may wish to brainstorm a list of potential subjects on your classroom whiteboard and then have the class vote on what they would like to draw. Or, you may choose to relate the drawings' subject to something you are studying in class or to a seasonal theme. Once you have chosen a subject, write it on a colored index card or sentence strip using a heavy black marker.

Hang a large sheet of chart paper on an easel and place it in front of the classroom or in your art center. Post the list of students' names next to the easel within easy reach. Then, place the index card or sentence strip naming the subject next to the easel.

Explain to students that they will take turns to make a big group drawing on the sheet of chart paper. When it is a student's turn, she will come to the easel, select a drawing tool, and add to the class picture. Then, she should use the pencil to mark her name off the list, read the next name, take the "your turn to draw" card to that student, and place the card on his desk. You may wish to have children draw during center time or at another time in the day. When it is the assigned time to draw, that child may complete his part of the drawing. He will deliver the card to the next student, who will take a turn to draw, and so forth.

When each child has had an opportunity to add to the group drawing, distribute an 11" x 17" (28 cm x 43 cm) sheet of paper to each student, along with crayons and pencils. Remind the children of the original subject of the group drawing and let them make individual drawings of the same subject.

Speaking, Writing & Sharing

Wrap up the lesson by displaying the group drawing in the center of a bulletin board with the individual drawings posted all around it. Gather your class near the bulletin board. First, talk about the group drawing and the things that are in it. If you wish, have individual children describe what parts they added to the drawing.

Then, select several students to talk about their individual drawings. Ask them to explain to the class how their drawings are like the group drawing and how they are different.

The Dot

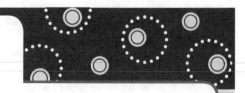

Written and illustrated by Peter H. Reynolds

Cambridge, MA: Candlewick Press, 2003

Story Summary

Vashti is a little girl who is having trouble getting started with her art project. Class is over and she is still sitting with a blank paper thinking that she cannot draw when her teacher encourages her to make a mark on the paper. Vashti makes a single dot with a jab from a marker, and her teacher has her sign it. The next week, Vashti returns to the classroom to see her little dot framed and hanging behind her teacher's desk. This inspires her to start making all kinds of different dots, any way she can. Finally, she exhibits all of her dots at the school art show. While there, she passes her teacher's encouragement on by telling a little boy to draw a line, which may start him on his own artistic journey. This book shows what a good teacher can do to encourage students and also points out how a little thing like a dot or a line may be all you need to start to do great things.

Literacy Concepts and Skills

- Describing
- Inferring
- Predicting
- Vocabulary—(descriptive words, strong verbs) empty, glued, leaned, blank, good, strong, jab, carefully, quietly, swirly, better, red, purple, yellow, blue, green, lots, little, many, big, bigger, splashed, splash, straight, shook, squiggle
- Writing

Art Concepts and Skills

- Collaboration
- Creative thinking
- Generating ideas
- Lines
- Painting, drawing, collage, etc.

Reading & Building Conversation

As you share the book with your class, use the following questions and prompts to encourage discussion and build oral language skills:

- At the beginning of the book, Vashti's teacher refers to Vashti's blank paper as "a polar bear in a snowstorm." Why would she call it that?
- Why do you think Vashti's teacher had her sign her dot? What do you think she is going to do with it?

- How do you think Vashti feels when she sees her dot framed in gold and hanging on the wall?
- While looking at the page showing the school art show, talk with the children about all the different dots featured and how Vashti made them.
- At the end of the book, Vashti tells the little boy to draw a line and sign his name. Why do you think she does that?

Creative Art Project •••••••••••••••••••••••••••••

There Are Many Ways to Make a Line

Materials

chart paper
marker
long roll of white butcher paper, about 2'
   (61 cm) high
scissors
school glue
markers
pencils
crayons
paint
paintbrushes
collage materials—assortment of ribbon, yarn,
   sequins, pasta shapes, colored paper, etc.

Process

Explore with your class the many ways to make a line. This is an open-ended project that is really only limited by you and your students' imaginations. First, have a brainstorming session with the children. On the top of a piece of chart paper, use a marker to write "How can we make a line?" Prompt your students to come up with different kinds of lines (straight, curved, wiggly, zigzag, etc.) and demonstrate how to make them. Also, list the different tools that could be used to make lines. Once the children have brainstormed lots of different things about lines, gather the suggested materials and others that they listed for the project.

Unroll about 10' (3 m) of butcher paper on the floor and set the art materials out on tables near the paper. Use a marker to write "Lines, Lines, Lines!" in large letters across the top of the butcher paper. Let several students at a time choose whatever materials they would like to use to create lines on the paper. They can select some sort of drawing instrument or paint to make a straight, wavy, spiral, curvy, or zigzag line. Or, they can use college materials to create lines from objects. Encourage students to spread out and use all of the available space on the paper.

Speaking, Writing & Sharing •••••••••••••••••••••

Once the line mural is complete and dry, hang it on the wall for display. Distribute copies of the My Line writing template (page 18) and have the children "write" or dictate something about their lines.

Name: _____

My Line

My line is _____ .

I made it with _____

_____ .

- -

Name: _____

My Line

My line is _____ .

I made it with _____

_____ .

Elmer

Written and illustrated by David McKee

New York: Lothrop, Lee & Shepard, 1968

Literacy Concepts and Skills

- Describing
- Predicting
- Sequencing
- Speaking
- Vocabulary—(colors, patterns, shapes, other descriptive words) young, old, tall, short, fat, thin, different, same, patchwork, yellow, orange, red, pink, purple, blue, green, black, white

Art Concepts and Skills

- Color
- Drawing
- Pattern
- Shapes

Story Summary

Elmer is an elephant who stands out from the crowd. Rather than being grey like the other elephants, Elmer is a patchwork of many different colors. Elmer keeps the other elephants laughing with games and jokes, but he is not happy because he is different. So, Elmer sets out through the jungle and finds a bush with elephant-colored berries. He rolls in the berry juice to turn himself elephant-colored. Now, he blends in with the other elephants, but no one notices him like they did before. The other elephants are silent and serious until Elmer finally plays a little joke. Just then, it begins to rain, and the berry juice washes off of Elmer, revealing his colorful patchwork. The other elephants laugh even more at what they think is Elmer's best joke ever. They decide to celebrate the day each year by decorating themselves with colorful patterns—while Elmer makes himself grey—and having a parade.

Reading & Building Conversation

As you share the book with your class, use the following questions and prompts to encourage discussion and build oral language skills:

- How is Elmer different from the other elephants in the book? How is he the same?
- What colors do you see on Elmer? What shapes do you see on him?
- What other animals does Elmer pass as he is walking through the jungle?
- Why does Elmer want to change his color?

- What do you think Elmer is going to do when he finds the bush with the elephant-colored berries? What happens to him?
- How do the other elephants act when Elmer returns to the herd?
- What do the other elephants do at the end of the book to make themselves more like Elmer? What colors, shapes, and patterns do you see on those elephants?

Creative Art Project ••••••••••••••••

Colorful Patterned Elephants

Materials

Elephant Cutout Pattern (page 21)
white card stock
scissors
crayons or markers

Process

Reproduce one elephant cutout on white card stock for each student. Either cut out the shapes or have students cut them out. Supply enough crayons or markers for children to share. Discuss the idea of patterns, pointing out the different patterns (flowers, dots, hearts, squares, stars, etc.) on the elephants in the last spread of the book. Have students color their elephants in patterns that they create.

Speaking, Writing & Sharing •••••••••••••••

Once students have finished their elephants, display them in a line on a classroom wall or bulletin board to create a colorful patterned elephants parade. Label the display "Elmer and the Elephants on Parade." Let children come forward and tell their classmates what colors, patterns, and shapes they used to decorate their elephants.

Elmer and the Elephants on Parade

Gingerbread Baby

Written and illustrated by Jan Brett

New York: G. P. Putnam's Sons, 1999

Literacy Concepts and Skills

- Describing
- Predicting
- Sequencing
- Speaking
- Vocabulary—(strong verbs) measured, mixed, rolled, popped, jumped, pranced, catch, reached, tumbled, twitched, sprang, rumbled, tumbled, caught, sniffed, wheeled, somersaulted, looked, winked, tiptoed, bouncing, twisted, strolled, trapped, backflipped, landed, bobbed, crept, licked, meddling, tweaked, followed, clapped, arrived, exclaimed, met, hear

Art Concepts and Skills

- Color
- Reading images
- Sculpture

Story Summary

Matti and his mother decide to bake a gingerbread boy on a cold winter day. But, Matti opens the oven too soon and a quick and mischievous gingerbread baby escapes. He runs out of the house and across the countryside, eluding people and animals as he goes. But, while Gingerbread Baby is running, Matti comes up with an idea to catch him. In the end, only Matti knows where Gingerbread Baby is.

Reading & Building Conversation

As you share the book with your class, use the following questions and prompts to encourage discussion and build oral language skills:

- Matti and his mother are planning to make a gingerbread boy, but instead they end up with a gingerbread baby. Why do you think that happens?
- Gingerbread Baby encounters and escapes from many different animals and people as he runs through the town. With your students, make an ordered list on chart paper of everyone he meets.

- Some pages in the book have illustrations on the sides showing what Matti is doing while Gingerbread Baby runs away. What is he making? Have your students predict what he may do with the thing he is making.
- The illustrations in this book are very detailed. To practice noticing visual details, choose one page in the book and let students talk as a group about everything they see.
- Where is Gingerbread Baby at the end of the story?

Creative Art Project

Clay Gingerbread Houses

Materials

House Cutout Pattern (page 24)
brown or terra-cotta self-drying clay, 2" (5 cm) diameter ball for each student
cardboard pieces, about 8" x 11" (20 cm x 28 cm) for each student, and additional pieces for house cutouts
waxed paper
rolling pins
plastic knives
plastic cups
water
tempera paint
paper plates (coated)
small paintbrushes
paper towels

Process

Trace the House Cutout Pattern onto several pieces of cardboard and cut out the shapes. Students will cut around the pattern shape with a plastic knife to create clay "gingerbread" houses.

Give each child a 2" (5 cm) diameter ball of clay, a plastic knife, a piece of cardboard, and a piece of waxed paper large enough to cover the cardboard. Show students how to put the waxed paper on top of the cardboard and then place the ball of clay in the center of it. Have a rolling pin and a house cardboard pattern for each group of several students to share. Demonstrate using hands and a rolling pin to flatten and roll out a ball of clay into a rough rectangle large enough to place the house pattern on. Show children how to lay the pattern on the clay and use the plastic knife to trace along the edges of the pattern to make a house shape.

Students can roll the extra clay into balls, snakes, and other shapes to place on their houses to look like candy. Provide cups of water for each group. Show them how to dip their fingers and spread small amounts of water on their clay shapes before sticking them to their houses. They may use the plastic knives to carve shallow lines for doors, windows, and other details. Once the houses are decorated, move the cardboard pieces to a safe place so that the houses can air-dry according to the instructions on the clay—often for one to two days.

Once the houses are dry, have children bring them back to their work areas. Set out cups of paint and water for cleaning brushes. Give each student a paper plate for mixing colors, several small paintbrushes, and a paper towel. Students may paint the decorations on their houses to resemble gingerbread houses.

Speaking, Writing & Sharing

When the painted houses are dry, have a sharing time. Invite children to come to the front of the class, show their houses, and explain why they think Gingerbread Baby would want to live there. Let them describe the shapes and colors they used to decorate their houses.

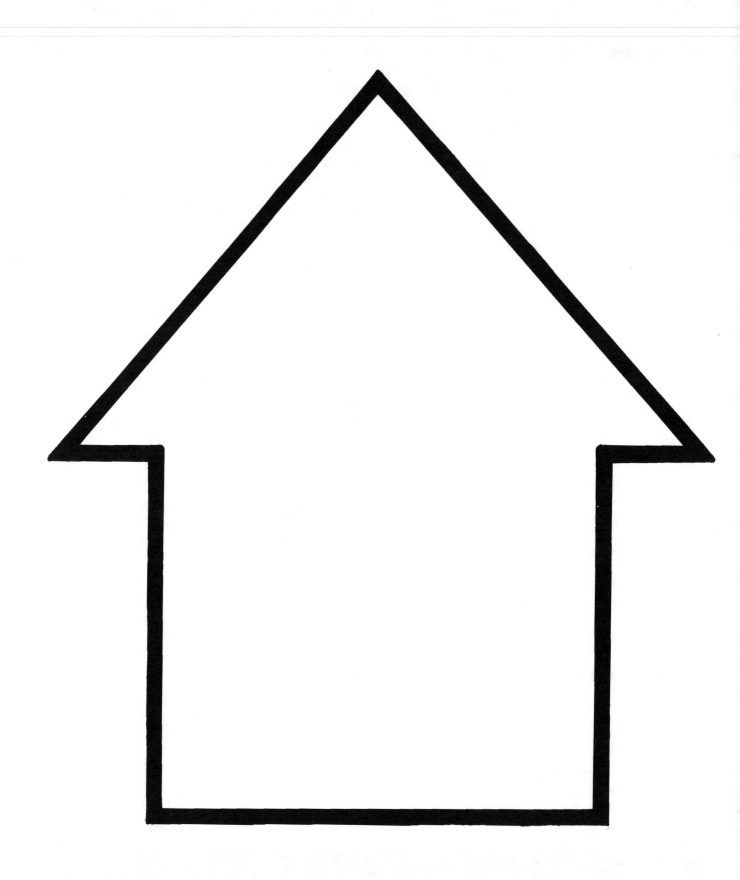

Harold and the Purple Crayon

Written and illustrated by Crockett Johnson

New York: HarperCollins Publisher, 1955

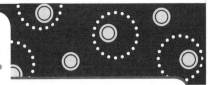

Literacy Concepts and Skills

- Describing
- Sequencing
- Speaking
- Vocabulary—(descriptive words, shapes) big, long, straight, short, small, tasty, frightening, terribly, fast, trim, quickly, sandy, nice, simple, nine, delicious, hungry, deserving, higher, farther, luckily, fine, front, whole, suddenly

Art Concepts and Skills

- Collaboration
- Drawing
- Line
- Shapes

Story Summary

In this classic book, Harold goes for a nighttime walk accompanied only by his purple crayon. As he walks, he constructs the world around him and creates his own story by drawing things with the crayon. The simple story and clean line illustrations, done in only black, white, gray, and purple, are a great basis for a group drawing project in which students imagine a new journey for Harold using line drawings in just one color.

ℝeading & Building Conversation

As you share the book with your class, use the following questions and prompts to encourage discussion and build oral language skills:

- What are some of the places Harold went on his walk? What are some of the things he did? If you were taking a nighttime walk like Harold, what are some of the places you would like to visit? What might you see in those places?
- Talk about the order of events in the book. Where did Harold go first? Next? And, where did his journey end? Encourage the use of sequencing vocabulary as your students discuss the story.

- The crayon Harold takes with him is purple. If you had to choose just one crayon to draw with, what color would it be and why?
- As Harold draws the things in his nighttime walk, he uses very simple lines and shapes to create the picture. Help your students identify the different shapes in the drawings (crescent, circle, triangle, oval, square, rectangle, star, etc.) and the different kinds of lines and marks (long, short, wiggly, wavy, straight, zigzag, dots, etc.).

Creative Art Project

Drawing a New Journey for Harold

Materials

roll of white butcher paper, about 2' (61 cm) tall and at least 10' (3 m) long
scissors
crayons in assorted colors, including black
Harold Cutout Pattern (page 27)
laminator or clear adhesive paper

Process

Reproduce, cut out, and laminate the cutout of Harold. Roll out enough butcher paper so that each student in your class has approximately 1' (30 cm) of space to draw in and cut it off the roll. Using a black crayon, draw a road that winds up and down the height of the paper, leaving space on each side of the road for student drawings. Explain to students that they are going to create a new journey for Harold by drawing the things and places he visits as he walks down the road on the paper.

During art or center time, let students come to the paper a few at a time, assign each student a section, and have them draw a place or thing Harold can visit as he walks down that part of the road. Each student may choose just *one color of crayon* for the simple lines and shapes used to create a drawing. If students need help coming up with places and things for Harold to visit, have a class brainstorming session and post ideas near the paper.

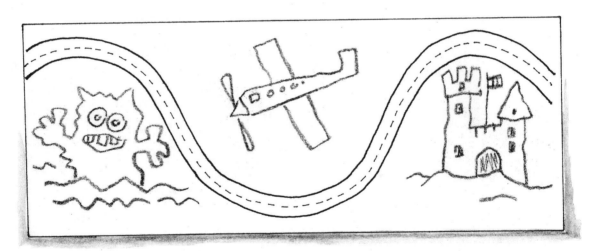

Speaking, Writing & Sharing

Hang the completed mural on the classroom wall or in a hallway. One at a time in order, let students come forward, take the cutout of Harold, and "walk" it to their drawings on the mural. When moving Harold down the road, each student can talk about the drawing, what Harold saw and did on that part of the journey, and what kinds of lines and shapes were used to make the drawing. Encourage the use of shape names and line vocabulary, such as *straight, curved, wavy, zigzag, short, long,* etc. As you review the mural with the class, also emphasize the use of sequencing vocabulary when discussing Harold's new journey.

26

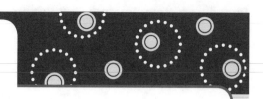

Hooray for Fish!

Written and illustrated by Lucy Cousins

Cambridge, MA: Candlewick Press, 2005

Literacy Concepts and Skills

- Describing
- Predicting
- Rhyming
- Speaking
- Vocabulary—(colors, shapes, other descriptive words) little, fishy, red, blue, yellow, spotty, stripy, happy, "gripy," "ele-fish," shelly, hairy, scary, (words used as adjectives for fish) eye, shy, fly, sky, fat, thin, twin, curly, whirly, twisty, twirly, upside down, round and round, many
- Writing
  .

Art Concepts and Skills

- Color
- Painting
- Patterns
- Shapes

Story Summary

Little Fish swims through the sea, introducing the many different fish along the way. The simple rhyming text describes these fish, some of which are loosely based on real fish and some of which are completely fantastic. Students learn many descriptive words and pick out an assortment of patterns and colors in the bold, simply painted illustrations during Little Fish's journey to find the most important fish in the world, Mama Fish.

Reading & Building Conversation

As you share the book with your class, use the following questions and prompts to encourage discussion and build oral language skills:

- There are multiple rhymes in the text of this book. On each page, have students identify the rhyming words.
- Many of the fish in this book have patterns such as dots, stripes, and swirls. Ask students to identify the shapes and patterns they see on the different fish.
- Look for the fish that have descriptive names reflecting how they look. Let students explain why a fish may have the name that it does.

- Ask children to identify some of the colors they see on the fish.
- There are many more fish in the book than the ones that are named. As you are reading, see if your students can find the fish listed below. To remind the children of what they are looking for, you may wish to write the following names on chart paper: pineapple fish, seahorse, peacock-tail fish, stingray, strawberry fish, white-starred fish, leaf fish, and heart fish.

Creative Art Project

Painting Big, Silly Fish

Materials

newspaper
large sheets of heavy paper, at least 11" x 17"
  (28 cm x 43 cm)
tempera paint in assorted colors
paper plates (coated)
large paintbrushes
plastic cups
water
paper towels

Process

Cover your work surface, whether tables or the floor, with newspaper. Give each student a large sheet of heavy paper, a paintbrush, a water cup, some paper towels, and a paper plate to use as a paint palette. Explain to children that they are going to paint their own fish based on the fish they saw in *Hooray for Fish!* Tell them to think about the different colors and the patterns they would like to make on their fish. Encourage them to paint their fish either as realistic or as funny as they want.

Speaking, Writing & Sharing

Once the paintings have dried, return them to the children. Ask your students to think about what they are going to name their fish. Give students sentence strips on which they can write their fish's names or scribe the names for them. Display the paintings with the fish's names on a bulletin board labeled "Hooray for Our Fish!"

Once all of the fish paintings are posted, let students come forward, identify which paintings are theirs, and tell the class their fish's names. Then, have the children talk about the colors and patterns they used in their paintings.

I Ain't Gonna Paint No More!

Written by Karen Beaumont

Illustrated by David Catrow

Orlando: Harcourt, 2005

Literacy Concepts and Skills

- Predicting
- Rhyming
- Vocabulary—(body parts) head, neck, chest, arm, hand, back, leg, feet

Art Concepts and Skills

- Collaboration
- Painting
- Tracing

Story Summary

A little boy is caught painting on the floor, ceiling, walls, curtains, and door of his house and gets in trouble with his mom, who tells him "Ya ain't a-gonna paint no more!" So, after a bath to clean up and a climb into the closet to retrieve his paints, he explains in infectious rhyming song how he "ain't gonna paint no more" as he proceeds to paint his entire body. You can chant the words to this book or sing them to the tune of "It Ain't Gonna Rain No More," but you are sure to have your students joining in with you as they guess which part of his body the little guy is going to paint next, up until the funny ending.

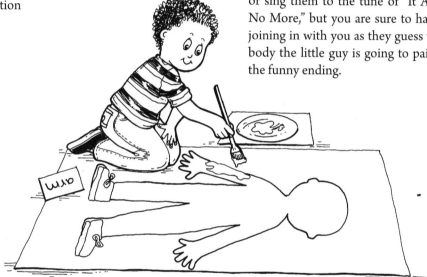

Reading & Building Conversation

As you share the book with your class, use the following questions and prompts to encourage discussion and build oral language skills:

- Find a recording of the traditional song "It Ain't Gonna Rain No More" and play it for your students. Then, when you read the book, you can sing the words to that tune.
- After the little boy's mom gives him a bath, she tells him that he ain't a-gonna paint no more and puts the paints on a high shelf. While on this page, ask your students what they think will happen next.

- As the little boy begins painting, he moves from body part to body part. On each page, have students predict what body part he is going to paint next. After a couple of body parts, they may notice two patterns: each body part rhymes with a word on the previous page and the boy moves from the top of his body to the bottom.
- Extend the lesson: Use the Word Cards on pages 32 and 33 to build vocabulary. Let children look at each card and name the body part that is highlighted by an arrow and a star.

Creative Art Project

Body Outline Painting

Materials

Word Cards (pages 32 and 33)
large roll of heavy white butcher paper, at least 2'
  (61 cm) wide
scissors
crayon or marker
tempera paints
paper plates (coated)
plastic cups
water
large paintbrushes
paper towels

Process

Divide your class into groups of two to four students. For each group, make a copy of the word cards on pages 32 and 33 on card stock. Set aside the word *body*. Place the remaining cards in a zippered bag.

Randomly choose one child in each group to have

his body outline drawn. On the floor, roll out white paper and cut off enough for the child to lay down on it. Let the child pose however he would like but suggest that he extend his arms and legs enough so that you can easily draw around them. Using a thick crayon or marker, draw around that child's body or, if possible, have one of the other children in the group draw the outline.

Provide each group with paints, along with one paintbrush for each color of paint and paper plates for color mixing. Let each child draw a card from the bag, "read" the word on it, and paint that portion of the outline any way the student would like. After one student finishes a body part, the next student draws a card and paints. Continue the process until all of the body parts in the outline have been painted.

Alternatively, pair up children so that they can draw each other's outline, or you draw the outline for each child. Then, let children paint their own outlines.

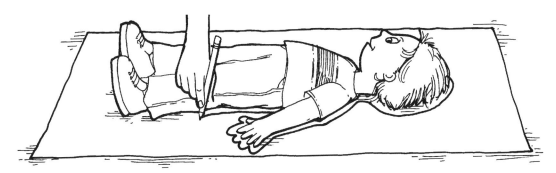

Speaking, Writing & Sharing

When the paintings have dried, display several of them at a time or, if you have enough room in your classroom or a hallway, all at once. Make cards with the names of different body parts on them, place adhesive putty on the backs of the cards, and hang them on the wall near the paintings. Invite students

to come up one at a time, choose a card from the wall, say the word on it, and place it on the correct spot on the student's painting. Provide all children with an opportunity to label at least one body part on their paintings.

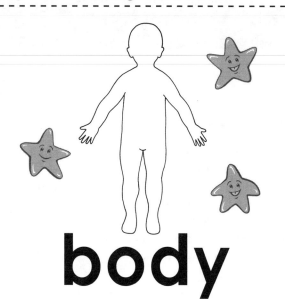

body

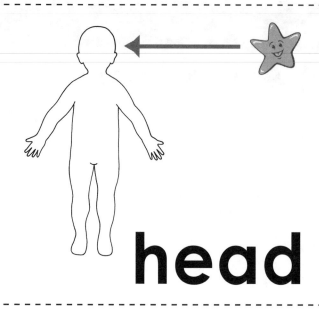

head

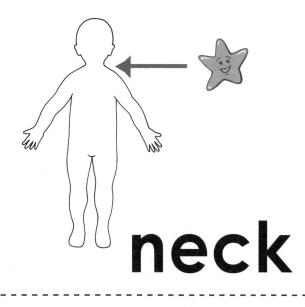

neck

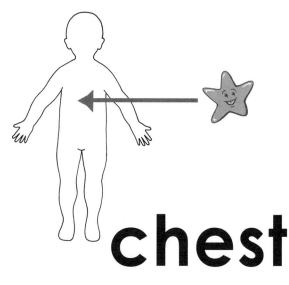

chest

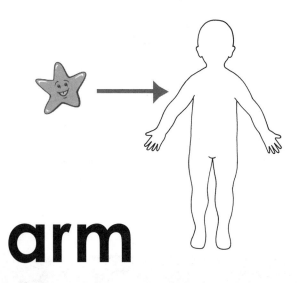

arm

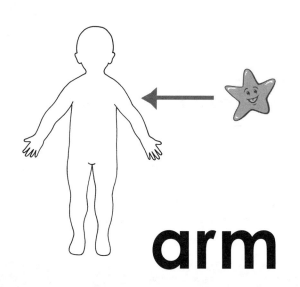

arm

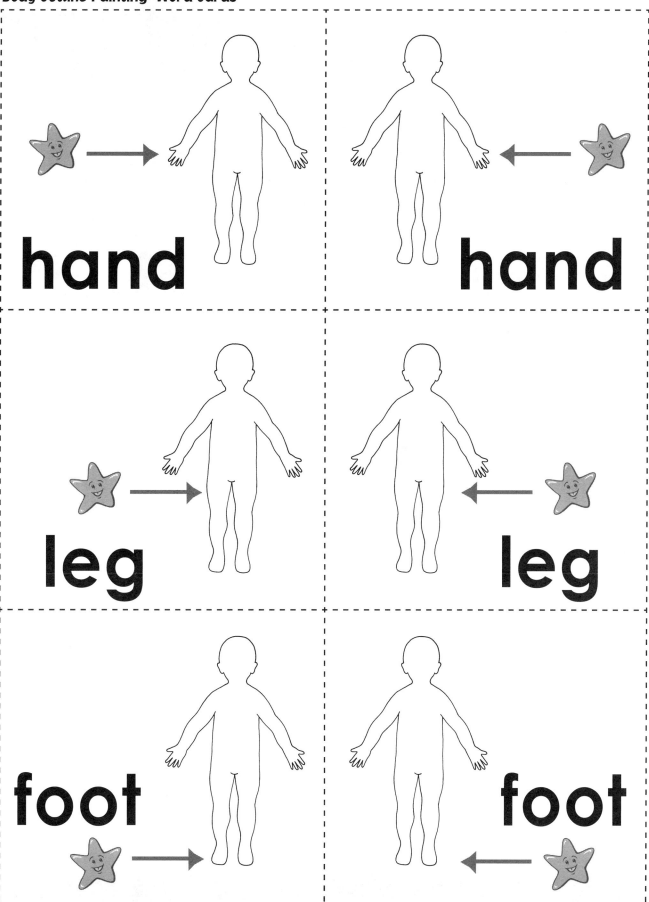

hand

hand

leg

leg

foot

foot

I Don't Want a Posh Dog!

Written and illustrated by Emma Dodd

New York: Little, Brown and Company, 2009

Literacy Concepts and Skills

- Describing
- Rhyming
- Vocabulary—(descriptive words) posh, blow-dry-when-washed, bouncy, jump-up-and-pounce-me, snooty, fancy, "attitudey," snappy, growly, never-happy, gruff, grunty, wheezy, tough, speedy, greedy, pleady, needy, itchy, "scritchy," scratchy, twitchy, silly, sweet, willy-nilly, not-too-proud, loud, know-me-in-the-crowd, always-ready-to-try
- Writing

Art Concepts and Skills

- Color
- Drawing
- Texture

Story Summary

A little girl talks about the kind of dog she wants, but she begins by telling what kind of dog she does not want. With descriptive rhyming text and expressive painted and collaged illustrations, this book introduces students to a fun variety of canine personalities. After reading, students think about what kinds of dogs they would like to have and draw their own dogs.

Reading & Building Conversation

As you share the book with your class, use the following questions and prompts to encourage discussion and build oral language skills:

- Some of the words that the little girl uses to describe dogs (such as *posh*, *pounce*, *snooty*, *gruff*, etc.) may be new to your students. As you read each page, let children use their own words to describe each dog. Then, tie the vocabulary in the book to the students' own descriptions.

- There are many rhymes in the text. Ask the class to identify rhyming words as you read.
- Each dog in this book has a different texture or pattern on its fur, plus there are other objects that incorporate distinctive textures. Ask children to describe how they think each dog's fur would feel based on the textures or patterns in the artwork.

Creative Art Project ●

My Kind of Dog

Materials

white drawing paper, 11" x 17" (28 cm x 43 cm),
one sheet for each student
crayons

Process

Tell your students that they are each going to make a drawing of the kind of dog they would like to have. Encourage them to think about how big or how small they would like their dogs to be, what color and texture of fur they would their dogs to have, and what kinds of things they would like to do with their dogs. Explain that the dogs can look realistic, or they can be silly and different.

Give each student a sheet of white drawing paper and have crayons available for all students. Encourage them to draw not just their dogs but also themselves doing the things they would like to do with their dogs.

Speaking, Writing & Sharing ● ● ● ● ● ● ● ● ● ● ● ● ● ● ●

Once children have completed their drawings, copy the writing template below and give one to each child. Have children each fill in a word or two to describe their dogs. Display the drawings with the completed templates on a bulletin board titled "Our Dogs."

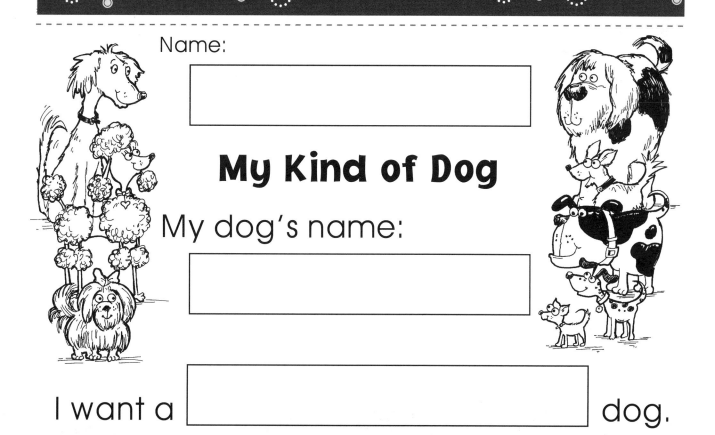

Name:

My Kind of Dog

My dog's name:

I want a ⬚ dog.

It Looked Like Spilt Milk

Written and illustrated by Charles G. Shaw

New York: HarperCollins Publisher, 1947

Story Summary

Sometimes "it" looked like spilt milk, a birthday cake, a rabbit, or a host of other interesting things. But, "it" isn't any of these things. Students will want to guess what "it" is as they look at the cut-paper collage illustrations and listen to the predictable text in this classic book.

Literacy Concepts and Skills

- Predicting
- Speaking
- Writing

Art Concepts and Skills

- Creative thinking
- Folding
- Printmaking
- Reading images
- Shapes

Reading & Building Conversation

As you share the book with your class, use the following questions and prompts to encourage discussion and build oral language skills:

- Read the first page of the book to students while showing them the facing picture to familiarize them with the text. Then, use self-stick notes or your hand to cover the words such as *Rabbit, Bird,* etc., on each of the following pages. Let the children look at the illustrations and guess what the objects are, removing the self-stick notes when they guess correctly.

- After you read all of the pages but the last one with your students, tell them that they will find out what "it" is on the next page. Have them predict what they think "it" is.
- As a follow-up activity, if possible, spend some time outdoors with your students looking at clouds in the sky and identifying the objects they see in the clouds. You may wish to let the children discover shapes in clouds after making their prints and filling in sentence strips like the example below.

Sometimes it looked like a heart.

Mandy

Creative Art Project ● ● ● ● ● ● ● ● ● ● ● ● ● ● ● ● ● ●

"It Looked Like . . ." Printmaking

Materials

black or dark blue construction paper, 9" x 12"
 (23 cm x 30 cm), one sheet for each student
white crayons
white tempera paint
plastic spoons
plastic cups

Process

Give each student one sheet of dark construction paper and a spoon. Have children write their names in white crayon on one side of their papers. Place cups with white tempera paint where each student can reach them.

Direct students to hold their papers with their names facing up. Then, show students how to fold their papers in half and reopen them so that there is a crease down the center. Have them take a spoonful of paint and "spill" it on one side of the crease. Next, tell students to fold their papers over on the crease and rub them to spread the paint. Finally, have them open their papers back up and allow the paint to dry.

Speaking, Writing & Sharing ● ● ● ● ● ● ● ● ● ● ● ● ● ●

Hang the prints on the classroom whiteboard or a bulletin board. One at a time, let students come forward, point to their prints, and tell the class what they think their prints look like. If they are not sure, you may ask for suggestions from the class. Once students have shared their prints with the group, have them fill in sentence strips with what they think their prints look like. Finish the sentence: "Sometimes, it looked like a . . ." Display the completed sentences with the prints.

Kiki's Blankie

Written and illustrated by Janie Bynum

New York: Sterling Publishing Company, 2009

Literacy Concepts and Skills

- Inferring
- Recalling details
- Role-play/performance
- Speaking

Art Concepts and Skills

- Collaboration
- Collage
- Drawing

Story Summary

Kiki is a little monkey who loves her polka-dot blankie. She takes it everywhere with her and uses it to make many things for her daily adventures. Kiki's blankie becomes a cape, a beach towel, a swimsuit, a tent, a napkin, and many other things. One day, Kiki goes sailing with her blankie as a sail and the wind blows the blankie away. It ends up on a tree branch above a sleeping crocodile. Upset, Kiki tries to figure out how to retrieve her blankie, but all of her ideas are things she thinks she cannot do without her blankie. Finally, she thinks of her blankie getting eaten by the crocodile, and she becomes very brave.

Reading & Building Conversation

As you share the book with your class, use the following questions and prompts to encourage discussion and build oral language skills:

- What does Kiki never go anywhere without?
- How does Kiki make her blankie into different things?
- What happens to Kiki's blankie while she is sailing? How does she feel when this happens?

- Why can't Kiki just walk up to her blankie and take it off the branch?
- Why do you think Kiki feels brave after she imagines the crocodile eating her blankie?
- How does Kiki finally get her blankie back?
- Think back through the story. What are some of the things Kiki makes from her blankie? What are some of the things she becomes while wearing her blankie?

Creative Art Project ● ● ● ● ● ● ● ● ● ● ● ● ● ● ● ● ●

What Can You Make with a Blankie?

Materials

6 or more lightweight blankets, at least 30" x 40"
  (76 cm x 102 cm)
fabric pieces, 4" x 6" (10 cm x 15 cm), one per
  student
school glue
white paper, 11" x 17" (28 cm x 43 cm)
crayons

Process

Your students will love using a real blanket, crayons, and fabric scraps to act out and create pictures of different things they can do with a blankie.

Divide students into pairs or small groups. Explain that you will give each group a blanket and that each group needs to be like Kiki and come up with one creative way to use the blanket. After the groups have time to formulate their ideas, have the groups take turns showing the rest of the class how they are using their blanket. The other students then guess what the blanket has become. Younger students may need to duplicate ways that Kiki uses her blankie, but some students may be ready to come up with new uses.

Once each group has demonstrated a way to use a blanket, students will create individual collages and drawings showing themselves using a blanket in an imaginative way. Before beginning, encourage students to think of what they are going to be in their pictures and how they are going to use their blankies to help them become that thing. Give each child a sheet of white paper, crayons, a piece of fabric to use as the "blankie," and glue.

Speaking, Writing & Sharing ● ● ● ● ● ● ● ● ● ● ● ● ●

Let volunteers come to the front of the room and show the class their blankie collages. Have the rest of the class guess what they are doing in the pictures and who or what they are.

Leaf Man

Written and designed by Lois Ehlert

Orlando: Harcourt, 2005

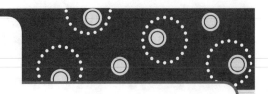

Literacy Concepts and Skills

- Describing
- Speaking
- Vocabulary—(descriptive words, types of leaves, seeds) blew, drifting, gliding, flying, following, traveling, lonesome, rustle, waiting, oak, acorn, ash, maple, maple seeds, sweet gum, sweet gum fruit, honey locust, ginkgo, catalpa, beech, hawthorn, linden, elm, birch, cottonwood, fig, poplar, horse chestnut

Art Concepts and Skills

- Collage
- Color
- Reading images
- Texture

Story Summary

On the first pages of this book, the narrator introduces Leaf Man, a figure made of leaves, acorns, and a sweet gum ball. He lived in a pile of leaves, but one day he blows away, leaving the narrator to track and wonder about his travels past animals, water, fields, and orchards. On each spread beneath beautiful illustrations made of collaged leaves, the narrator describes what Leaf Man may be seeing. Your students will love following along where Leaf Man goes and identifying the pictures that the leaves form. The endpapers of the book explain how the author created the artwork for the book (the illustrations are actually made from color photocopies of leaves!) and provide labeled examples of many different kinds of leaves.

Reading & Building Conversation

As you share the book with your class, use the following questions and prompts to encourage discussion and build oral language skills:

- When you are reading the first two pages of the book, ask your students to show you where Leaf Man is. Have them point out what makes up his head, body, arms, legs, hands, feet, eyes, and nose and mouth. If you wish, discuss the types of leaves that make up these body parts. (Use the endpapers of the book as reference for different kinds of leaves.)
- As you read each spread of the book, let children point out pictures or figures that they see in the illustrations made from leaves. Some things are mentioned in the text and some are not. As they discuss the images, have them describe the colors, shapes, and textures of the leaves and other objects they see.
- Another feature of this book is the treatment of the tops of the pages. As you turn each page, ask students to look at the top of the page and talk about its shape. This is a good opportunity to reinforce vocabulary like *smooth, wavy, bumpy, zigzaggy, jagged*, etc.
- This book contains several terms, such as *meadows* and *orchards*, which may be unfamiliar to students. On these pages, pay special attention to identifying what is in the illustrations to help students develop an understanding of these words.

Creative Art Project •••••••••••••••••••••••••••••••••••

Leaf Pictures

Materials

zippered plastic bags
assorted leaves, seeds, nuts, etc.
fall-colored construction paper, 9" x 12"
(23 cm x 30 cm), one for each student
school glue
paper plates (coated)

Process

First, collect enough leaves and other natural materials for each child to create a leaf picture. You may do this by going on a nature walk as a class, by collecting leaves as a group on your playground, or by having children collect them at home. Give each of your students a zippered plastic bag to hold the leaves and other materials that they collect.

If you wish, work with your students to identify the kinds of leaves they have collected. You can use the images on the endpapers of *Leaf Man* to do some of the identification.

Once each of your students has a bag of leaves, give them each a sheet of construction paper and a paper plate with white glue on it. Discuss some of the different pictures that the author made using leaves, and explain that they may create pictures or abstract patterns. Show students how to dip their fingers into the glue and smear it generously on the leaves. Encourage them to use enough glue to hold their leaves on their papers securely.

Speaking, Writing & Sharing •••••••••••••••••••

When the leaf pictures are dry, display them on a bulletin board with the title "Our Leaf Pictures." Invite several students to come forward to talk about their pictures, identifying what is in each picture, what kinds of leaves were used, and the picture's colors and textures.

Leonardo the Terrible Monster

Written and illustrated by Mo Willems

New York: Hyperion Books for Children, 2005

Story Summary

Leonardo is a little monster who couldn't scare anyone. He compares himself to other monsters who have no trouble frightening people and is disappointed in himself. He decides to find the most scaredy-cat kid in the whole world so that he can at least scare one person. After some research, Leonardo decides on Sam, who he thinks will be very easy to scare. But while trying to scare Sam, he discovers that it is better just to be a wonderful friend than a terrible monster.

Literacy Concepts and Skills

- Describing
- Speaking
- Vocabulary—(body parts) teeth, hands, toe, foot, eyes, head, tummy; depicted in illustrations of monster: teeth, claws, horns, eyes, ears, tails, antennae, tongue
- Writing

Art Concepts and Skills

- Assemblage
- Drawing
- Sculpture

Reading & Building Conversation

As you share the book with your class, use the following questions and prompts to encourage discussion and build oral language skills:

- What does Leonardo look like? Do you think he is scary? Why or why not?
- What do the other monsters in the book look like? What special body parts help make them scary? Do you think they are scary? Why or why not?

- What does Leonardo do to try to be scary? Who can show the class how Leonardo acts?
- What does Sam do when Leonardo tries to scare him? Why does he do that?
- What does Leonardo decide he wants to do instead of being a terrible monster?
- Would you like to have a monster as a friend?
- What would you like your monster to look like?

Creative Art Project

Making a Paper Lunch-Sack Monster

Materials

paper lunch sacks, one for each student
newspaper
stapler
crayons or markers
construction paper scraps
yarn and other assorted collage materials
scissors
school glue
paper plates (coated)

Process

Give each of your students a brown paper lunch sack. Show them how to make a monster body by tearing off large pieces of newspaper, crumpling them up, and placing them inside the sack to make it stand up. Fold over and staple the top of each sack shut.

Set out paper and other collage materials, along with scissors and paper plates with glue. Have students cut out body parts (such as heads, hands, feet, horns, or whatever parts they want their monsters to have) from construction paper scraps and glue them on their sacks. They can also use yarn to create hair or fur, and decorate their monsters' bodies using crayons or markers.

Speaking, Writing & Sharing

Once children have finished their paper bag monsters, display the artwork on shelves throughout the classroom. Give each child a copy of the My Monster writing template (page 44). Have students write or dictate their monsters' names in the first box on the template, *He* or *She* in the second box, and what makes their monsters scary in the third box. During sharing time, let several students come forward, show their classmates their monsters, and "read" what they wrote about their monsters.

43

Name:

My Monster

My monster's name is _____ .

_____ is scary because
(He/She)

_____ .

- -

Name:

My Monster

My monster's name is _____ .

_____ is scary because
(He/She)

_____ .

The Little Scarecrow Boy

Written by Margaret Wise Brown
Pictures by David Diaz

New York: HarperCollins Publishers, 1998

Literacy Concepts and Skills

- Describing
- Predicting
- Rhyming
- Speaking
- Vocabulary—(body parts shown in the illustrations) tongue, fingers, mouth, teeth, lips, nose, eyes, ears

Art Concepts and Skills

- Assemblage
- Color
- Collage

Story Summary

The little scarecrow boy so wants to be able to go out into the field with his father, old man scarecrow, to help him scare the crows away. But, his father tells him over and over again that he is not fierce enough to scare a crow and that he must grow. Every evening, old man scarecrow teaches the little scarecrow boy the six fierce faces he must learn to scare the crows. One day, after he has learned all six faces, the little scarecrow boy decides to run away to the field to try to scare the crows. He begins to make all six faces, each one fiercer than the one before, but has no success until the sixth and final face. He then sees his father's shadow, who has been watching proudly as he made all six faces. With his father's help, the little scarecrow boy grows up to become the fiercest scarecrow in the entire world. This book presents a great lesson about being patient until a person is old enough to tackle a task and the fact that parents will be there for their children as they are learning new things.

Reading & Building Conversation

As you share the book with your class, use the following questions and prompts to encourage discussion and build oral language skills:

- What does the little scarecrow boy want to do with his father?
- Why does his father tell him he cannot do that?
- How many different fierce faces does old man scarecrow teach his son?
- What do you think will happen when the little scarecrow boy goes into the field by himself?
- Ask students to look at the illustrations and describe each of the little scarecrow boy's six fierce faces. Have them use body part vocabulary to describe how the scarecrow boy is using his face and hands to make the faces.
- What happens when the little scarecrow boy tries to scare the crows with his first five faces?
- What happens when he tries to scare the crows with his sixth face?
- Have students identify the rhyming words in the chant old man scarecrow says to his son each day. Chant: "No, little boy. You can't go. You're not fierce enough to scare a crow. Wait till you grow."

Creative Art Project

Fierce Scarecrow Faces

Materials

paper plates (uncoated), one for each student
assorted colors of construction paper
collage materials—string, yarn, buttons, etc.
craft sticks (jumbo size)
crayons
school glue
scissors

Process

Give one paper plate to each student. Provide them with collage materials, scissors, crayons, and glue to create fierce scarecrow faces on their plates. Talk about what a fierce scarecrow face might look like. Discuss the parts that their fierce faces could include, such as eyes, nose, mouth, hair, a hat, etc. Optional: Attach a large craft stick to the back of the plate to make it easier to hold.

Speaking, Writing & Sharing

Once students have finished creating their scarecrow faces, have them take turns coming up to share the faces with the class. Invite them to tell their classmates what about the faces makes their scarecrows fierce and what actions their scarecrows do to scare away crows.

Minerva the Monster

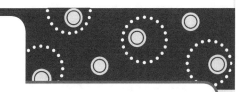

Written and illustrated by Wednesday Kirwan

New York: Sterling Publishing Company, 2008

Literacy Concepts and Skills

- Describing
- Making connections
- Speaking
- Vocabulary—(action words when Minerva is making her mask) drew, taped, colored; (action words when Minerva is a monster) roared, rumbled, tramped, pounced, stomped, hung upside down, snarled, ate, crashed, bellowed, grunted, growled

Art Concepts and Skills

- Assemblage
- Color
- Sculpture

Story Summary

Minerva is a little dog who is having a wonderful time pretending to be a monster. She asks her mom to help her make a monster costume. After creating a paper-plate monster mask, she spends the rest of the day doing monster things like pouncing at birds, stomping leaves, and growling at her baby sister. But, Minerva discovers that a monster doesn't get to do many of the things that a little girl dog likes to do, and she decides at the end of the day that she prefers being Minerva—or maybe a tiger. This book provides a great opportunity for students to describe actions, to talk about the things they like to pretend to be, and to create their own monster masks.

Reading & Building Conversation • • • • • • • • • • • • •

As you share the book with your class, use the following questions and prompts to encourage discussion and build oral language skills:

- Minerva likes to pretend to be many different things. Do you like to pretend? What kinds of things, people, or animals do you pretend to be? What do you do while you are pretending?
- What does Minerva's monster look like? Describe how she looks when she is a monster.
- What are some of the things Minerva's monster does? Describe how Minerva acts when she is a monster.

- If you were a monster, what would you look like and what would you do?
- When Minerva's father tells her that monsters live in dark caves without anyone to read to them, what does Minerva imagine? What do the monsters she imagines look like? While looking at the monsters on this page, have your students describe them.
- Why does Minerva decide she no longer wants to be a monster?

Creative Art Project

My Own Monster Mask

Materials

paper plates (uncoated), one for each student
pencil
stapler
narrow elastic pieces, 12" (30 cm) for each student,
    or craft sticks (jumbo size)
collage materials—assortment of paper, yarn,
    sequins, fabric, etc.
crayons or markers
school glue
scissors

Process

Hold a paper plate up to each of your students' faces, use a pencil to mark where to cut the eyeholes, and then cut them out for the students. Cut an approximately 12" (30 cm) length of elastic for each mask and staple one end of it to each side of the mask so that it will stay on the student's face. Alternatively, attach a craft stick for holding the mask.

Set out the glue, scissors, collage materials, and crayons or markers. Direct children to first think about how they would like their monsters to look. Then, invite them to use any of the collage materials and crayons or markers to make the monster masks.

Speaking, Writing & Sharing

Once students have finished their masks, have a monster parade around the classroom. Help students put on their masks if needed, play some fun or scary music, and march or dance around the classroom for a few minutes. After the parade, ask for volunteers to come forward, show the rest of the class their masks, and talk about their monsters. Have brief interviews with the "monsters," asking them their names, to describe how they look, and to talk about some of the things that they like to do.

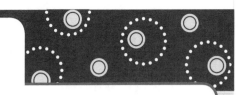

Mouse Paint

Written and illustrated by Ellen Stoll Walsh

San Diego: Harcourt Brace & Company, 1989

Literacy Concepts and Skills

- Predicting
- Speaking
- Vocabulary—(colors, other descriptive words, verbs) white, red, yellow, blue, thought, climbed, dripped, stepped, stirred, orange, hopped, mixed, green, jumped, splashed, purple, sticky, stiff, soft, painted
- Writing

Art Concepts and Skills

- Color
- Painting

Story Summary

There are three white mice who live on a white piece of paper where the cat cannot find them. One day, while the cat is sleeping, they find three jars of paint: red, yellow, and blue. Deciding this is Mouse Paint, the mice climb right in and paint themselves. While splashing around in the puddles they create, they discover how to mix these colors to make orange, green, and purple. After they clean themselves off, they paint on paper using the three colors they have and the three colors they can make. They even remember to leave one portion of the paper white so that they can still hide from the cat.

Reading & Building Conversation • • • • • • • • • • • • • •

As you share the book with your class, use the following questions and prompts to encourage discussion and build oral language skills:

- Where do the mice in the story live? Why?
- The mice drip puddles of paint onto their paper, and they think those puddles look like fun. What do you think they are going to do in the puddles?
- The mice step into puddles that are different colors than they are and begin to do a little dance. Let students predict what will happen when each mouse dances in a puddle.
- What colors are the three mice? What colors do they make when playing in the paint, and how do they make them?
- What happens when the mice paint their paper different colors? Does it make the mice easier or harder to see?
- Why do the mice leave one part of their paper white?

Creative Art Project

Mixing Mouse Colors

Materials

Mouse Colors Reproducible (page 51)
cotton balls
paper plates (coated)
newspaper
red, blue, and yellow tempera paint
white drawing paper

Process

Make two copies of the Mouse Colors Reproducible for each child. Cover the work surface, whether tables or the floor, with newspaper. To start the activity, provide each student with six (or more) cotton balls, one copy of the Mouse Colors handout, and a paper plate with separate blobs of red, yellow, and blue paint. Fill in the color words (*red, yellow,* and *blue*) on the handout. Tell students that they are going to paint using their little white "mice" (the cotton balls). Show them how to dip a ball into just one color and dab it into the mouse outline labeled with that color name, using a new "mouse" for each color. Explain that the colors on their plates and on the handout are called primary colors, which means that they cannot be made by mixing other colors together. Once children have completed the Mouse Colors handout, distribute a second copy of the reproducible to each child. This time, fill in the color words *orange, green,* and *purple*. Explain to students that they will make these three colors, known as secondary colors, by mixing two primary colors together. Ask them what two colors they will mix to make orange. Have them use their cotton balls to mix that paint color in the corresponding labeled mouse. Repeat the steps to make the colors green and purple. Explain to the children that they may need to make their mice "dance around" (smearing two colors together) in the mouse outlines to create the new colors.

Once students have filled in the drawings of mice, give them a sheet of white paper to paint anything they like using their cotton ball mice. Remind the children to use each mouse only in the same color as before if they want to keep their colors separate.

Speaking, Writing & Sharing

When the paintings are dry, select several students to come forward, show their artwork to the class, and describe what they painted and the colors they mixed to create the colors in their paintings.

Mouse Colors

Make each mouse a different color.

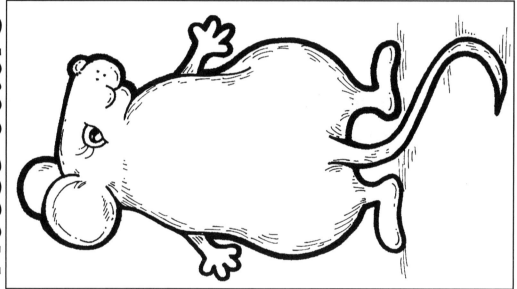

Color:

Color:

Name:

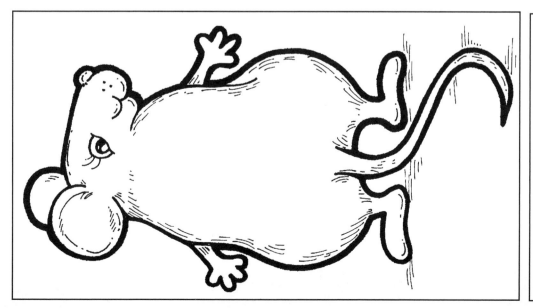

Color:

Not a Box

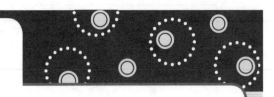

Written and illustrated by Antoinette Portis

New York: HarperCollins Publishers, 2006

Literacy Concepts and Skills

- Describing
- Making connections
- Predicting
- Role-playing/performance
- Writing

Art Concepts and Skills

- Collaboration
- Drawing

Story Summary

The simple line illustrations and words in this book tell about a little rabbit playing with a cardboard box. On each page, the narrator asks why the rabbit is doing a specific thing with the box. Then, on the next page, the rabbit explains that it is NOT a box, and the illustration shows what the rabbit is pretending the box is. The simple text in the book is fun for students to predict, and they will have a great time describing the different things the rabbit is doing with the box.

Reading & Building Conversation

As you share the book with your class, use the following questions and prompts to encourage discussion and build oral language skills:

- Have you ever played with a large cardboard box? What are some of the things you made from it or pretended it was?
- For each "box" page, let students describe what the rabbit is doing to or with the box.

- When you read each "not a box" page, ask your students to identify what the rabbit is pretending to do with the box.
- The text in this book is very predictable. After the first couple of pages, see if your students can predict what the words on the next page will be.

Creative Art Project

Your Own "Not-a-Box"

Materials

one or more very large cardboard boxes
brown construction paper, 9" x 12" (23 cm x 30 cm), one sheet for each student
black crayons or markers

Process

Place the box at the front of your classroom. To prepare for this art project, your students will be role-playing with the box. One or two at a time, invite children to come forward and pantomime something they would do with the box. Have the rest of the class guess what they are doing and what they are imagining the box to be.

Once every child has had a chance to play with the box, distribute the pieces of brown construction paper. Using just black crayons or markers, have students draw themselves and a "Not-a-Box" on their papers, showing what they are imagining their boxes to be and how they are playing with them. Have them think about the illustrations in *Not a Box* while they draw.

Speaking, Writing & Sharing  • • • • • • • • • • • • • • • • •

When the children have finished their drawings, display them on a "Not-a-Box" bulletin board. You may wish to display the class's own "Not-a-Box" nearby.

Give each of your students a copy of the writing template below and have them write or dictate a word to complete the sentence. Hang the template below each student's "Not-a-Box" drawing.

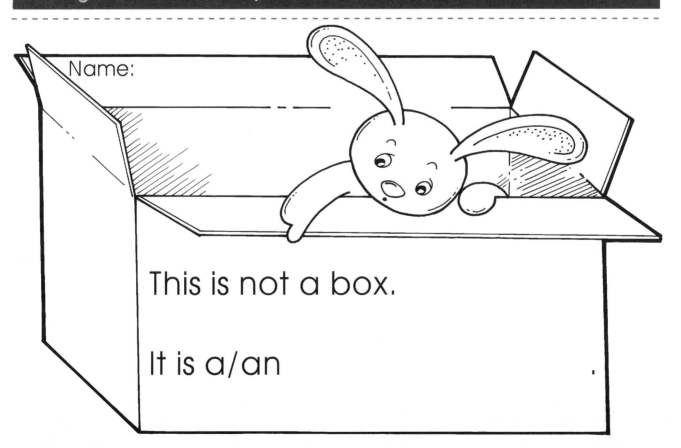

Name:

This is not a box.

It is a/an

Secret Seahorse

Written by Stella Blackstone

Illustrated by Clare Beaton

Cambridge, MA: Barefoot Books, 2004

Literacy Concepts and Skills

- Rhyming
- Speaking
- Vocabulary—(descriptive words) secret, deep, down, quick, bright, flickering, shrugged, steadily, ancient, dark, dim, shivered, glint, whole; (depicted creatures) anemone, angelfish, barracuda, clownfish, crab, hermit crab, lion fish, giant clam, jellyfish, lobster, octopus, oyster, parrotfish, sea slug, sea turtle, sea urchin, shark, starfish, stingray, swordfish
- Writing

Art Concepts and Skills

- Collage
- Reading images
- Texture

Story Summary

In this book, swim with the narrator who is looking for a seahorse in a coral reef. The book explores many different creatures and places, but the elusive seahorse continues to hide on the two-page spreads. Finally, at the end, the narrator—and reader—discover an entire family of seahorses. The beautiful illustrations are made of stitched fabric collages with accents of beads, sequins, lace, rickrack, buttons, yarn, and other interesting materials. The simple rhymes in the text and the chance to hunt for the seahorse on each set of pages will engage children throughout the book. Included for the reader are several pages of information on the different coral reef sea creatures shown in the illustrations.

Reading & Building Conversation

As you share the book with your class, use the following questions and prompts to encourage discussion and build oral language skills:

- Have children find the secret seahorse in each illustration. Watch out! There are two spreads where no part of the seahorse can be seen.
- As you read each page, let children identify the sea creatures they see on that page. If they are not sure about one, check to see if it is included in the information at the back of the book.

- On each page, have students identify the different materials they see in the illustrations. Have them describe the textures of the materials or how they think they would feel if they could touch them. Words they may choose to use include *soft, rough, bumpy, smooth, stringy,* etc.
- The text in this book is a simple rhyme describing the pursuit of a seahorse. As you pause throughout your reading, ask students to identify the rhyming words in the text.

Creative Art Project

My Secret Seahorse

Materials

Seahorse Cutout Pattern (page 56)

white card stock, 8.5" x 11" (22 cm x 28 cm)

assorted collage materials, including fabric, felt, yarn, lace, sequins, plastic jewels, and beads

scissors

school glue

paper plates (coated)

Process

Copy the Seahorse Pattern onto white card stock. Give each child a copy of the seahorse to cut out. Lay out the collage materials, scissors, and paper plates with glue. Explain to children that they are each going to create a secret seahorse by choosing pieces of collage materials and gluing them to the seahorse shape. Show them how to attach the fabric and the other materials to the seahorses using the glue. When the work is complete, lay the decorated seahorses aside to dry.

Speaking, Writing & Sharing

Once the seahorse collages are dry, have a Secret Seahorse Hunt in your classroom. Give each child a copy of My Secret Seahorse Clues (page 57). Let children hide their seahorses around the room. Then, have them "write" or dictate two or three clues for finding their seahorses on the reproducible.

When your students have completed their clues, have them come forward one at a time and read the clues aloud so that classmates can hunt for the seahorse. After each seahorse has been found, let the child talk about how it was decorated, naming the materials that were used and its textures.

Name:

My Secret Seahorse Clues

1.

2.

3.

Tails

Written by Matthew Van Fleet

Orlando: Harcourt, Inc., 2003

Story Summary

Combining a simple rhyme describing the characteristics of different animals' tails and cute animal images with textures, *Tails* will have your students reaching to touch and feel it. Be sure to plan time during the book's reading for children to touch, feel, and manipulate its pages. Many of the animals are familiar to students, but there are several that may be new to them. To help with identification, there is an illustration near the back of the book labeled with all of the animals' names.

Literacy Concepts and Skills

- Predicting
- Rhyming
- Vocabulary—(descriptive words) furry, spiny, rainbow-hued, shiny, stand up, drag, frisky, fluffy, stringy, scaled, strong, clingy, long, stumpy, grumpy, old, new, bumpy, cool, hot, swishing, broad, slinky, stinky, large, small, biggest
- Writing

Art Concepts and Skills

- Collage
- Drawing
- Texture

Reading & Building Conversation

As you share the book with your class, use the following questions and prompts to encourage discussion and build oral language skills:

- Look at the cover of the book with your students. After reading the book's title, ask them what they think the book is going to be about.
- Before opening the book to its first page, point to each of the tails in the title. Ask students to describe the texture of each tail, and let them try to identify what kind of animal each of the tails belongs to. Open the front cover to reveal the animals and confirm their guesses.

- As the children examine the animals' tails, have them use different adjectives from those given in the book to describe how the tails look or feel.
- Let students describe other things about the animals, such as whether they are big or small, what color they are, and what other interesting body parts they have.
- Each two-page spread in this book contains a brief verse that rhymes. After you read each spread, ask students to identify the rhyming words on the pages.

Creative Art Project

Furry Tails

Materials

white paper, at least 8.5" x 11" (22 cm x 28 cm), one sheet for each student

crayons or markers

collage materials with different textures— assortment of fabric, fake fur, felt, yarn, shiny or textured paper, sandpaper, etc.

scissors

school glue

paper plates (coated)

Process

Give each student one sheet of drawing paper and lay out the drawing and collage materials, scissors, and glue on paper plates where your students can reach them. Explain that they are going to draw an animal and glue materials on their drawings to give their animals special tails like the ones in the book. Each tail can have an unique texture, or students can choose to give the tails specific shapes. Let children select any animal they like and to be creative in choosing the textures for their animals' tails.

Speaking, Writing & Sharing

Once students have completed their collages, work with them to write sentences about their pictures. Make one copy of the following sentence on a sentence strip for each child: "My _____ has a _____ tail." To show how the sentence will be finished, write the following example on chart paper: "My <u>monkey</u> has a <u>curly</u> tail." Explain that students will fill in the first space with the name of the animal and the second space on the sentence strip with a word describing the animal's tail. Give each student a prepared sentence strip. Have the children "write" or dictate words to complete the sentences. Display the collages with the corresponding sentences nearby.

"My monkey has a curly tail."

The Very Busy Spider

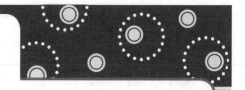

Written and illustrated by Eric Carle

New York: Philomel, 1984

Story Summary

Early one morning the wind blows a spider onto a fence post near a farmyard, where she begins to spin a web. The animals on the farm try to distract her from her work, but she keeps busily spinning until she finishes. Finally, the rooster asks her if she wants to catch a fly, and that's just what she does in her newly completed web. After her busy day, the spider falls asleep. The illustrations are made of painted paper collages with a wide variety of textures and patterns on them, along with raised-line drawings of the spider's web and body. As you read this book, be sure to have your students look at the lines in the spider's web and touch them to feel their texture.

Literacy Concepts and Skills

- Predicting
- Speaking
- Vocabulary—(animal sounds and names) neigh, horse; moo, cow; baa, sheep; maa, goat; oink, pig; woof, dog; meow, cat; quack, duck; cock-a-doodle-doo, rooster; whoo, owl; (descriptive words) thin, silky, pesty

Art Concepts and Skills

- Collage
- Color
- Drawing
- Lines
- Shapes
- Texture

Reading & Building Conversation

As you share the book with your class, use the following questions and prompts to encourage discussion and build oral language skills:

- Read the first few pages of the book, pausing after the words "The spider didn't answer." Invite students to guess why she did not answer the animal.
- The text in this book follows a predictable pattern. After reading the first few pages, have your students chorus the words "The spider didn't answer; she was very busy spinning her web."
- The spider and her web are printed using a textured ink that students can feel; on each page, give one or two children the opportunity to touch the spider and web and describe it.
- The spider's web is made up of different kinds of lines; have students talk about what kinds of lines they see in the web (possibilities include straight, angled, up and down, curved, and crossed).
- The spider's web and the fence she builds it on create different kinds of shapes. On several pages, let the children describe what shapes they see (possibilities include rectangles, triangles, and other irregular shapes).
- The artwork in this book is made of collages of painted paper; the paper often has different textures and patterns on it. Let students describe textures or patterns they see on the animals (possibilities include spots, splatters, and speckles and curly, swirly and furlike strokes).
- Have the children repeat the sounds that the different animals in the book make.

Creative Art Project ·

Sparkling Spider Webs

Materials

Spider Cutout Pattern (page 62)
scissors
crayons
dark colored construction paper,
  one sheet for each student
pencils
white school glue in bottles
silver glitter
shaker bottle with small holes
funnel
flat box with an open top (large enough for the
  construction paper to sit flat in it)

Process

Copy the Spider Pattern so that each student has one spider. Let students color their spiders as they wish with crayons and then cut them out.

Using a small funnel, pour silver glitter into a shaker bottle. Give each child a sheet of paper and explain how to create a spider web with glue and glitter. First, have students use pencils to sketch their spider webs on their papers. Encourage them to create different kinds of lines such as straight, curved, and wavy. Then, show children how to squeeze lines of glue over the pencil lines. While the glue lines are still wet, sprinkle the web drawings with glitter. Do this by placing each glued drawing in the box and helping the child shake enough glitter onto the drawing to cover the glue completely. Then, pick up the web drawing and shake the excess glitter into the box. Set the drawing aside to dry.

After every few students shake glitter onto their drawings, scoop up the excess glitter that has accumulated in the box and use a funnel to pour it back into the shaker.

Once the glue on the spider webs is dry, let children glue their decorated spiders onto their spider webs.

Speaking, Writing & Sharing · · · · · · · · · · · · · · · · ·

Display the completed drawings on a bulletin board titled "Our Very Busy Spiders." One at a time, invite students to talk about their spider webs, telling the class what kinds of lines and shapes they used. Have the children also describe what their spiders look like, including what colors the spiders are.

Sparkling Spider Webs—Spider Cutout Pattern

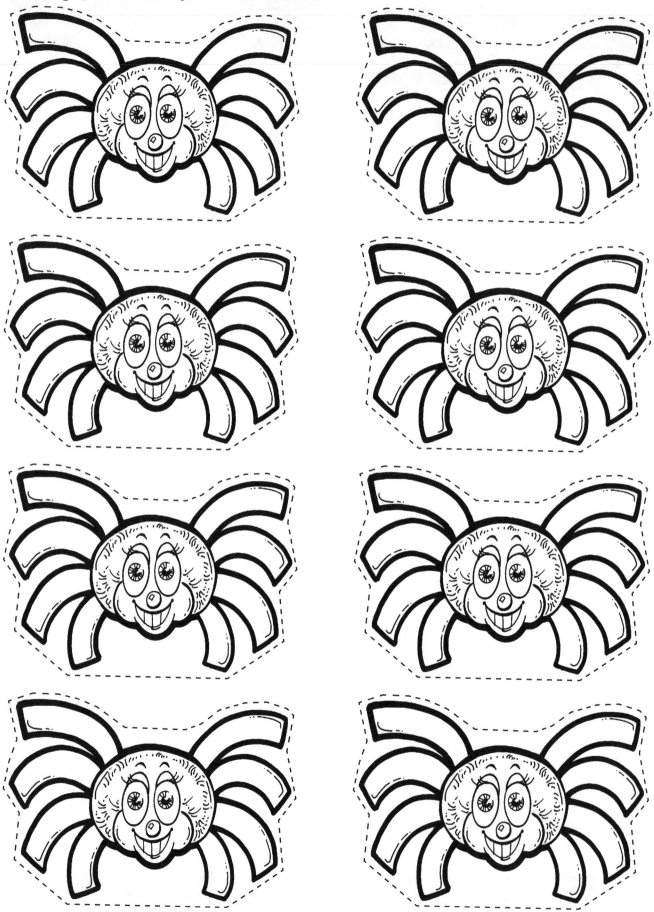

Correlations to NAEYC/IRA Position Statement, the NCTE/IRA Standards & National Arts Standards

Read, Talk & Create! supports the following recommendations from *Learning to Read and Write: Developmentally Appropriate Practices for Young Children,* a position statement of the National Association for the Education of Young Children (NAEYC) and the International Reading Association (IRA). This resource also supports the National Council of Teachers of English (NCTE) and International Reading Association *Standards for the English Language Arts* and the *National Standards for Arts Education.*

NAEYC/IRA Position Statement *Learning to Read and Write: Developmentally Appropriate Practices for Young Children*

The activities in this book support the following recommended teaching practices for preschool students:

1. **Adults create positive relationships with children by talking with them, modeling reading and writing, and building children's interest in reading and writing.**

    Read, Talk & Create! supports this teaching practice by providing teachers with conversation prompts, writing activities, and art activities that build student interest in reading and writing.

2. **Teachers provide and draw children's attentions to print-rich learning environments.**

    The resource book contains many ideas for displays that contribute to a print-rich learning environment.

3. **Teachers read to children daily, both as individuals and in small groups. They select high-quality, culturally diverse reading materials.**

    Each unit in *Read, Talk & Create!* begins with a teacher reading a picture book to the students.

4. **Teachers provide opportunities for children to discuss what has been read to them, focusing on both language structure and content.**

    Each unit in *Read, Talk & Create!* includes discussion prompts teachers use to promote conversations about the books they have read to their students.

5. **Teachers provide experiences and materials that help children expand their vocabularies.**

Each picture book featured in *Read, Talk & Create!* presents new vocabulary to students.

Certain activities in this book support the following recommended teaching practices for kindergarten students:

1. **Teachers read to children daily and provide opportunities for students to independently read both fiction and nonfiction texts.**

    Each unit in *Read, Talk & Create!* begins with a teacher reading a picture book to her students.

2. **Teachers provide opportunities for students to write many different kinds of texts for different purposes.**

    The resource book includes a variety of writing activities.

3. **Teachers provide writing experiences that allow children to develop from the use of nonconventional writing forms to more conventional forms.**

    Several writing activities offered in this book use writing templates that support students in moving toward conventional writing. In addition, teachers are encouraged to allow students to dictate their writing projects if they are not yet able to write on their own.

4. **Teachers provide opportunities for children to work in small groups.**

    Several of the art projects in *Read, Talk & Create!* are designed for small groups.

5. **Teachers provide challenging instruction that broadens children's knowledge of their world and expands their vocabulary.**

    Each picture book featured in *Read, Talk & Create!* presents new vocabulary to students.

NCTE/IRA *Standards for the English Language Arts*

The activities in this book support the following standards:

1. **Students read many different types of print and nonprint texts for a variety of purposes.**

   Each unit begins with the teacher reading a picture book with students. The children also practice examining and interpreting the artwork in the picture book.

2. **Students use a variety of strategies to build meaning while reading.**

   Discussion prompts and writing projects in *Read, Talk & Create!* focus on such reading skills as predicting, reading for details, sequencing, comparing and contrasting, inferring, describing, developing vocabulary, and making connections, among others.

3. **Students communicate in spoken, written, and visual form, for a variety of purposes and a variety of audiences.**

   While doing the activities, students communicate verbally through class discussions and presentations, in writing through a variety of writing projects, and visually through art projects in various media.

4. **Students become participating members of a variety of literacy communities.**

   The group discussions and group art projects in *Read, Talk & Create!* help teachers build a classroom literacy community.

National Arts Standards

This book supports the following visual arts content and achievement standards for K–4 students from the *National Standards for Arts Education*:

Content Standard 1: Understanding and applying media, techniques, and processes

Achievement Standards:

- **Students know the differences between materials, techniques, and processes.**

  Students use a wide variety of materials and techniques to do the art projects in *Read, Talk & Create!*

- **Students describe how different materials, techniques, and processes cause different responses.**

  For selected projects in *Read, Talk & Create!* students discuss the art they have created.

- **Students use different media, techniques, and processes to communicate ideas, experiences, and stories.**

  Students use a variety of materials and techniques to communicate ideas in their art projects.

Content Standard 2: Using knowledge of structures and functions

Achievement Standard:

- **Students use visual structures and functions of art to communicate ideas.**

  Students communicate ideas about their chosen subject in each art project in *Read, Talk & Create!*